Contents

Houses	3
The streets	5
Tradespeople	6 – 7
"Rags and bones!"	8 – 9
Shops	10 – 11
The cinema	12 – 13
"Eating out"	14 – 15
Trams, trolleys and buses	16 – 17
Factories	18 – 19
Out of work	20 – 21
Special events	22 – 24

Rosebery Avenue, London 1934

Houses

Sunbury, Surrey

This photograph shows houses built in the 1930s. They were built along main roads leading out of town. They are called semi-detached houses because they are joined together in pairs. Most of the houses look alike. Only the more expensive houses had room for a garage.

Look at this photograph of a street in the 1930s. Look for:
— the small garden in front of each house. There was also a garden at the back.
— the striped poles at the pedestrian crossing. Lights flashed on these to warn drivers. What are pedestrian crossings like now?

"It was lovely to have
a newly-built flat to ourselves.
For the first time in our lives
we had a bathroom. But we had
to pay more rent than before."

The first council flats were built
in the 1930s. These children are
playing outside the flats where they
live. They have no playground or
garden to play in.

Portsmouth

Things to do

Start to make a book about town life in the 1930s.
Call the first page *Houses*.

Draw pictures of any town houses which were built in the 1930s.
They will probably be away from the town centre.
Draw another picture of the house or flat in which you live.
Is it different from those shown in the photographs?

Find out if there are any council houses or flats near where
you live which were built in the 1930s.

The streets

This is a photograph of a busy town street taken over 50 years ago.

Look for:

— the two trams
— the man driving the horse and cart
— the shops with their blinds to keep out the sun
— the stalls in the road, outside the shops
— the people in the street
— the advertising signs on the shops.

What else can you find in the picture?

Hoe Street, Leyton, London 1930

"Often we had no money to spare for tram fares to the town, so we walked both ways."

"Sometimes, on a cold winter evening, we bought hot chestnuts from the man who roasted them on his barrow. We warmed our hands on them before we ate them."

In the 1930s there was less traffic in the town streets than now. But the trams took up a great deal of room. People had to walk out to the centre of the street to get on them.

"I remember the water cart used to come round in hot weather and spray the streets to make them cool."

Things to do

Find someone who lived in a town during the 1930s. Ask them to tell you about the streets. What was the traffic like then? Write in your book what they tell you.

Draw a picture of a street 50 years ago.

Tradespeople

"The grocer came to our house every Friday.
He took away with him the order for next Friday's groceries."

"The baker came three times every week.
As well as bread, he sold cakes, pies and sausage rolls."

Few people had cars in which to go shopping. Many tradespeople brought their goods to people's homes. The grocer, the greengrocer, the butcher, the baker and the fishmonger all had delivery vans. Some were pulled by horses.

Gillingham, Kent 1938

Look at the delivery van in the photograph.
What shop does it come from? What has the driver brought to the house?
What do you think he will take away?

This man cycled round the streets selling ice cream. People called him the "Stop Me and Buy One" man.
Look for:

— the box "fridge" in which the wrapped ices were kept
— the notices on the front of the box. How much did the ices cost?
— the man's uniform.

"If we wanted him to call at our house we put a card in our window. It had a large W (for Wall's) **on it."**

People at home had no freezers so they were pleased to see the ice cream seller. He rang his bicycle bell to let everyone know he was coming.

Things to do

Make up a conversation between the driver and the woman at her door.

Draw a picture of the "Stop Me and Buy One" man. Make a list in your book of the ice creams he sold. Do ice cream sellers come into your street? What do they drive? How do they let you know they are there?

Write about any tradespeople who deliver things to your house.

"Rags and bones!"

"I remember the rag-and-bone man calling out as he came down the street with his hand cart. People looked in their cupboards and drawers to see what they could find for him."

Not all tradespeople who came round the streets were selling things.

The man in this photograph is offering to take things away.
People called him the "rag-and-bone man".

8

"Sometimes he would give us three pennies for some clothes, or twopence for a rabbit skin. When I was a child he once gave me a balloon for an old saucepan."

Look again at the photograph.
Look for:

— the rag-and-bone man. How is he dressed?
   What do you think he is calling out?
— his hand cart. Notice the large wheels and the two legs
   on which it stands.
— the load on his cart. What has he collected so far?

The rag-and-bone man took almost anything which he thought he could sell: old clothes, books, rabbit skins, old tin kettles, pans and baths.
He paid very little for them.

Things to do

Draw a picture in your book of the rag-and-bone man.

Ask someone over 60 if they remember the rag-and-bone man calling. Did they give him anything? What did he give them in return? Write down what they tell you in your book.

Does anyone come down your street buying or selling things? How do you know they are there? What do they sell? What do you do with things you don't want?

Shops

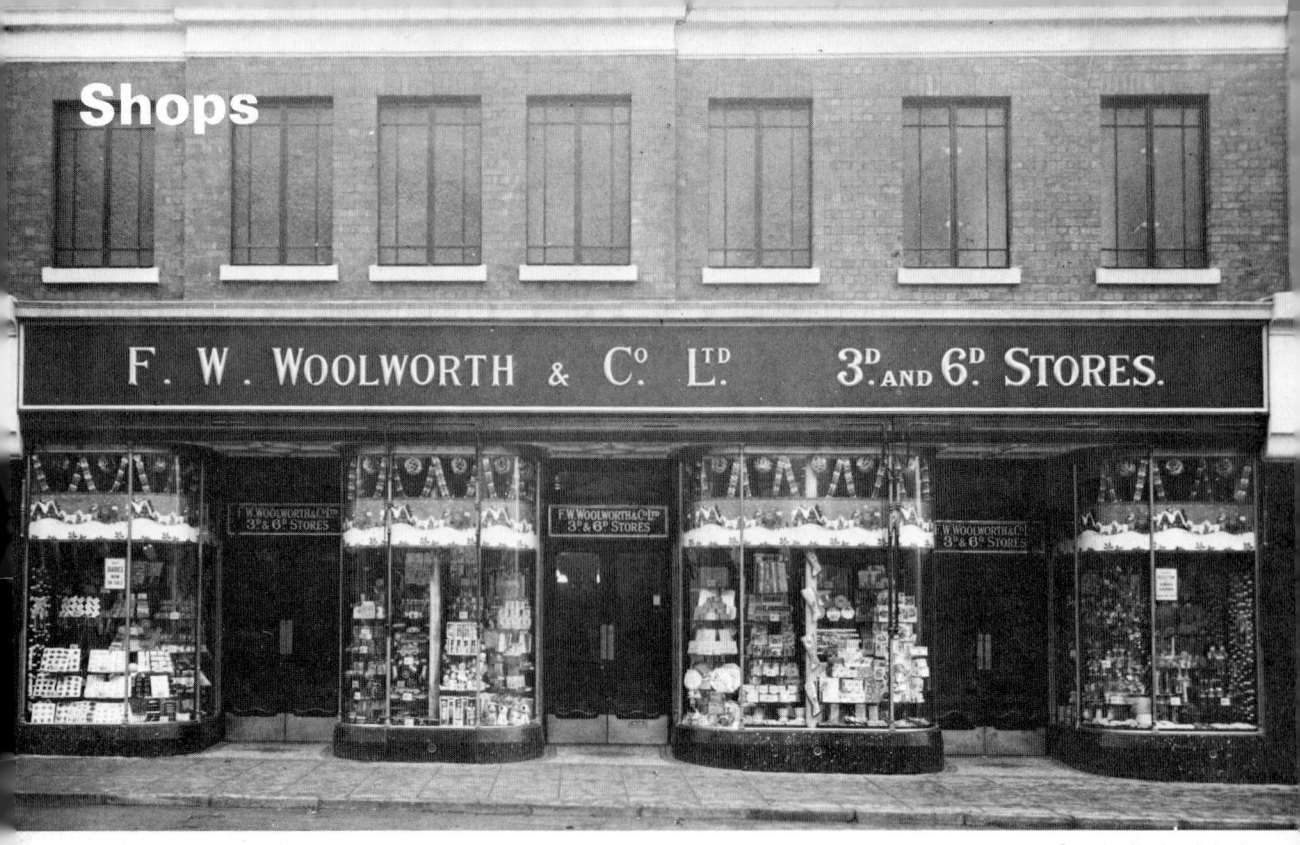

Coleraine, Northern Ireland

**"My grandad bought a pair of spectacles.
He paid sixpence for each lens and sixpence for the frames.
He tested his eyesight by reading a card at the counter."**

Most large towns had a shop like the one in the photograph, where "nothing cost more than sixpence ($2\frac{1}{2}$p)". Cans of food, packet groceries, sweets, ice cream, toys, books, records, household equipment, hardware and electrical fittings were some of the many goods sold at low prices.

Chain stores, like Marks and Spencer's, International and Lipton's, began to open shops in many towns.

People could buy factory-made clothes at low prices. A new suit cost about 50 shillings (£2.50).

The people in the photograph below are doing their Christmas shopping at chain stores.

"On a cold day we loved to walk round the warm shops without being asked to buy anything."

Things to do

Talk to someone older than 60. Ask them to tell you about shopping in the 1930s. Where did they buy their clothes? How much did their clothes cost?

Draw a picture of someone shopping 50 years ago. Look carefully at the photographs to see what clothes they wore.

The cinema

Eros News Theatre, London 1938

"All the week we looked forward to our visit to 'the pictures'. There were usually two long films, a cartoon and the news. The programme often lasted over three hours."

Stepney, London

Every town had at least one cinema. Some were like huge palaces, like the one in the photograph. Look for:

— the tall pillars
— the patterned walls and ceiling
— the many bright lights.

"Best of all, we loved the deep throbbing sound of the organ as it rose slowly in front of the screen. After he had finished playing, the organist turned and waved to us as he sank down again beneath the floor."

Savoy Cinema, Hayes, Middlesex 1937

This is a poster for a popular film of 1935.

Things to do

Is there a cinema in your town? What is its name? Try to find out if it was there in the 1930s.

Ask someone older than 60 about going to the cinema in the 1930s. What films did they see? What tunes did the organist play? Write down what they tell you.

Draw a picture of the organist *or* people queuing outside a cinema in the 1930s.

"Eating out"

"Sometimes we went to a teashop after a visit to the cinema or the shops."

Almost every town had its teashops, where friends could meet to enjoy a pot of tea, some toasted teacakes and a plate of assorted "pastries", or cakes, for a shilling or two.

The Strand Corner House, London

This photograph shows one of the London "Corner Houses", which were very popular eating places in the 1930s. Inside the entrances, flowers, cakes, chocolates and other confectionery were sold.

Each floor had its own type of restaurant where people could enjoy a meal and listen to an orchestra in pleasant surroundings.

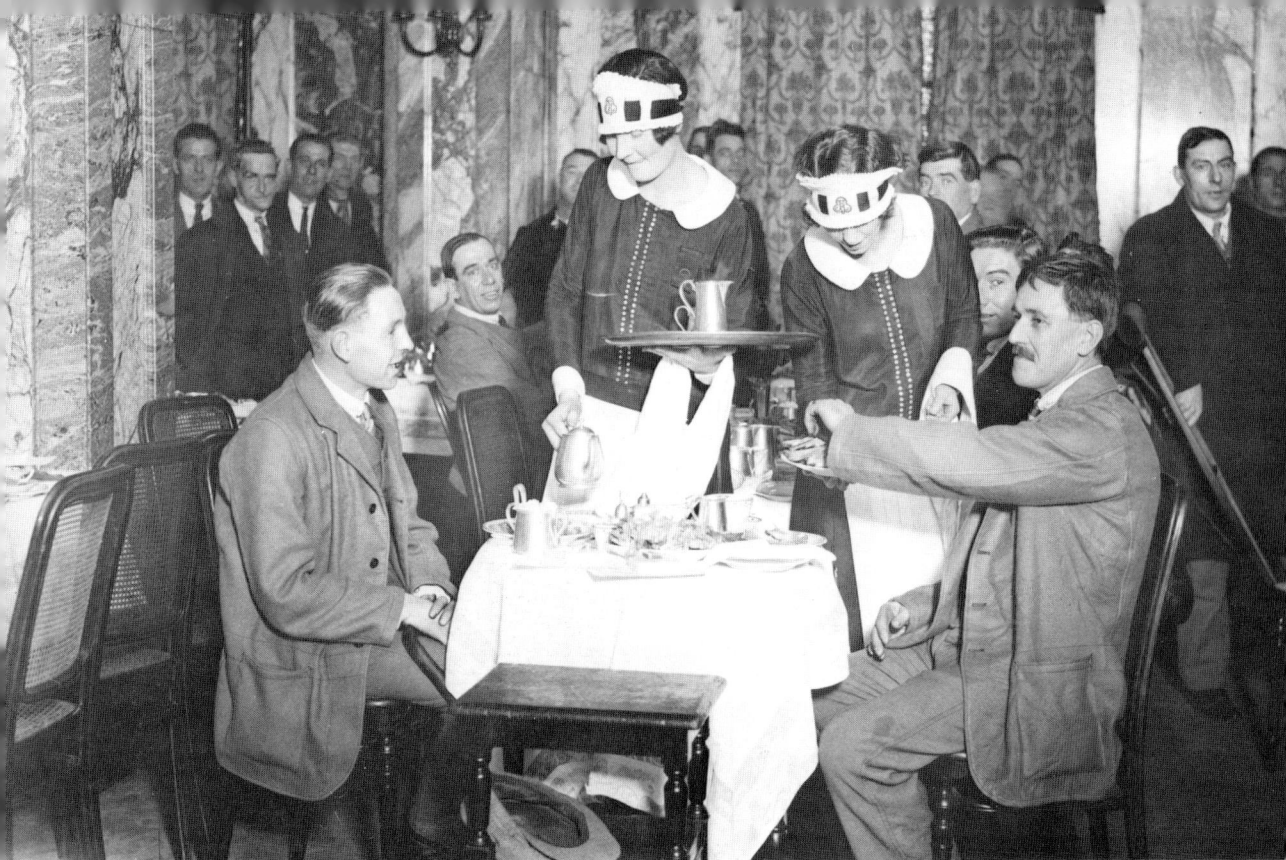

Lyons' Corner House, Coventry Street, London 1926

This photograph shows the inside of one of the "Corner House" restaurants. Look at the waitresses, who were called "Nippies". They were famous for their neat appearance and quick, pleasant service.

Things to do

Talk to someone over 60 and ask them if they ever went to a Corner House. Write down in your book what they tell you.

People "eat out" more often today than in the 1930s. Write about a meal you have enjoyed in a café or restaurant.

Trams, trolleys and buses

South Shields, Tyne and Wear

"We sat on hard wooden seats upstairs and we were rocked about as the tram went along. The driver sounded a bell with his foot. It went 'clang! clang!' and warned everyone to keep out of the way."

Many towns had trams like the one in the photograph. They ran on railed tracks and worked from an electricity supply which passed overhead. Look for:

— the tram driver with his hands on the controls
— the passengers sitting upstairs and downstairs.

Durham 1930

Some towns had electric trolley buses instead of trams.
They needed no tracks and were more comfortable.

Motor buses fetched people into the town from their homes to work, or to do shopping. Look at the single-decker buses in the photograph.
Look for:

— the drivers and conductors
— the queue of passengers.

Things to do

Draw a picture of a street with some traffic in the 1930s.
Remember to include some horse-drawn vehicles.

Talk to someone over 60. Did they travel on a tram?
What did it sound like? Was it a smooth ride? Write down in your book what they tell you.

Factories

Many new factories were built in the 1930s. Most of these were in the south of England.

The Pyrene Co. Ltd factory, London 1930, where fire extinguishers were made

"We only had a short time to do our work before it moved on for the next job to be done by someone else."

Inside the factory, workers stood in a line at assembly belts. These girls are working in a biscuit factory. Why did they keep their hair covered?

W & R Jacob Co. Ltd, Liverpool 1926

Dagenham, Essex 1934

This is a photograph of Ford's new car factory in the 1930s. Look for the long row of cars being put together. The cars moved slowly forward all the time. Each worker fitted a particular part to the cars. In this way, cars could be made more quickly and more cheaply than before.

In 1935 a Ford car cost £100. Thousands of families could afford to buy their first car. People used their new cars mainly for weekend trips into the country, and for going on holidays.

"When we first drove into London, Dad couldn't reverse the car. We had to get out and push to turn it round."

Things to do

Is there a factory near where you live which was built in the 1930s?
Find someone older than 60 who once worked there.
Ask them what things the factory made.

Collect pictures of cars made in the 1930s. Talk to someone who owned a car at that time. How did they learn to drive? Where did they go? Write down what they tell you in your book.

Out of work

Many people were unable to get work in the 1930s. In some areas in the north of England over half the workpeople had no jobs. They had very little money on which to live.

"I was an out-of-work miner on the north east coast. I used to walk along the beach each morning and pick up pieces of coal which had been washed up by the tide. The salt from the sea made it burn brightly on the fire."

In this photograph out-of-work miners are taking home sacks of coal on their bikes. They have picked up pieces of coal from the slag or rubbish heap at the colliery. It was a slow, dirty and tiring job. Look for:

— the heavy sacks balanced across the bikes
— the hill up which the bikes have to be pushed.

This man has hired a barrel organ for the day. He is taking it round the streets. It cost him from a shilling (5p) to half a crown (12$\frac{1}{2}$p).

When he stopped, he put his cap down on the pavement. He hoped people passing by would put some coins in it. Sometimes he walked round all day and was given only a few shillings.

Stepney, London 1933

Look again at the photograph.
Look for:

— the man's cap, scarf and shabby overcoat
— the waterproof cover to keep the barrel organ dry when it rained
— the lamp which had to be lit after it became dark.

Things to do

Find out all you can about barrel organs and the tunes they played. Perhaps you can find one in a museum.

Ask someone older than 60 if they had a job in the 1930s. Did they know other people who were out of work? Write down what they tell you.

Special events

"Every Saturday night we went dancing at the Empress Hall. It held 500 people and cost a shilling (5p) **to get in.**"

Wigan 1939

"Everyone in the street joined in. We all had a wonderful time."

In the photograph below people are having a street party, to celebrate the coronation of King George VI and Queen Elizabeth. It was 12 May 1937. Parties like this were held in almost every town and village in the land.

Coronation spoon 1937

Look for:

— the flags and many other decorations
— the people of all ages at the party
— the paper hats

Things to do

Talk to someone older than 60. Can they remember the name of a 1930s dance band? What popular tunes did the dance bands play? Write down what they tell you.

Pretend you are at the party in the photograph. Write about what happened after tea. Draw a picture about it.

Ask someone who remembers when our present Queen was crowned to tell you what happened in their street or town.

London 1939

"It was the first time I had ever been away from home."

"I kept wondering where I would sleep that night."

In this photograph children and their teachers are being evacuated from a school in London in 1939.
War had begun between Britain and Germany and air raids were expected.
Do you think you would have liked going away from home?

The following museums have displays about life in the towns in the 1930s:

The Museum of London, London Wall
North of England Open Air Museum, Beamish Hall, Stanley, County Durham
The Tramway Museum, Crich, near Matlock, Derbyshire
London Transport Museum, Covent Garden, London

Museum of Transport, Albert Drive, Glasgow, Scotland
Castle Howard Costume Galleries, Castle Howard, York
National Motor Museum, Beaulieu, Hampshire